IT'S TRUE!

SPORT
STINKS

IT'S TRUE!

Did you know that frogs are cannibals,
fashion can be fatal and the dinosaurs
never died? Or that redheads were
once burned at the stake as witches?
Find out why rubbish tips are like lasagna,
and how maggots help solve crimes!

Books to make
your brain bulge!
find out all about them on
www.itstrue.com.au

JUSTIN KEMP & DAMIAN FARROW
PICTURES BY HEATH McKENZIE

IT'S TRUE!
SPORT
STINKS

ALLEN&UNWIN

First published in 2006

Allen & Unwin
83 Alexander Street
Crows Nest NSW 2065
Australia
Phone: (61 2) 8425 0100
Fax: (61 2) 9906 2218
Email: info@allenandunwin.com
Web: www.allenandunwin.com

National Library of Australia
Cataloguing-in-Publication entry:

Kemp, Justin.
It's true! sport stinks.
Bibliography.
Includes index.
For children.
ISBN 978 174114 854 1.
ISBN 1 74114 854 5.
1. Sport – Juvenile. I. Farrow, Damian.
II. McKenzie, Heath. III. Title. (Series: It's true; 24)

Series, cover and text design by Ruth Grüner
Cover photograph: Henrik Sorensen/Getty Images
Set in 12.5pt Minion by Ruth Grüner
Printed by McPherson's Printing Group

1 3 5 7 9 10 8 6 4 2

**Teaching notes for the It's True! series are available
on the website: www.itstrue.com.au**

CONTENTS

WHY SPORT?

Have you ever wanted to know what tricks Shane Warne has up his sleeve to take so many wickets? Or how Sharelle McMahon became such a sharp shooter? Or why Lance Armstrong keeps winning the Tour de France?

You might be surprised to discover that science can help answer these questions.

When we were kids we both wanted to be sporting superstars. There was just one thing standing in our way – we weren't all that good. But we were really good at science, so we combined our love of sport with our need to know *why* and *how*, and we became *sports scientists*.

Now we get to do experiments with sports stars to discover the secrets behind their success. We analyse games to understand the tactics of the winning team. And we even get to help athletes break world records by inventing better ways of training.

But every now and then, when no one's watching, we still pretend to be sporting superstars!

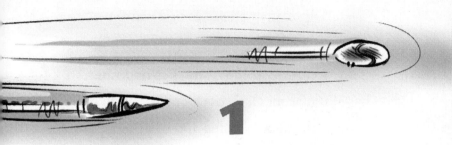

1

BLINK AND YOU'LL MISS IT

'Keep your eye on the ball!' Every coach and parent says it. Meanwhile you're thinking that the ball is zipping by far too fast to see. Well, science agrees with you. It's true! Even sports stars have trouble keeping their eyes on the ball.

TENNIS TELEPATHY?

Tennis star Andy Roddick serves the ball at over 200 kilometres (124 miles) per hour. That's almost as fast as a Formula One racing car zooms around the track.

At that speed, Andy's ball takes less than half a second to reach the other end of the court. The opposing player has about as much time as it takes you to blink to decide where the ball is going and what sort of shot to play, to get in to position, and to swing the racquet. There just isn't enough time for all that.

If you're a champion tennis player you have to prepare your shot before the ball has even left the server's racquet!

ANDY'S BALL WOULD TAKE:

- ▶ 8 seconds to go round an athletics track.
- ▶ 13 minutes to finish a marathon.
- ▶ 4.4 hours to travel from Sydney to Melbourne.
- ▶ 72 days to reach the moon.

Does this mean you have to be a mind-reader to be good at tennis? Should your coach be telling you to keep your eye on a crystal ball instead? Well, champion tennis players are more like 'body-readers' than mind-readers. Someone like Serena Williams watches the way the server tosses the ball and reads the angle of their body and arm to predict where the ball will go. You could call it good guessing or tennis magic – take your pick.

What about you?

If you just like to have a hit-up with your mates, do you still need tennis magic?

Your opponent serves at around 80 kilometres (50 miles) per hour, that's 20 metres (22 yards) per second, you only have just over a second to respond.

FEROCIOUSLY FAST BOWLERS

Cricket players also have to be good body-readers. Australian fast bowler Brett Lee can send the ball down the pitch at 150 kilometres (93 miles) per hour. When he lets go of the ball he is only 20 metres (22 yards) away, so the batsman has about as much time as a tennis player to decide what to do.

Australia's most famous batsman, Sir Donald Bradman, was a master at reading body language. 'The movement of the hand and arm gives the first clue as to the bowler's intentions,' he said. No wonder he had such an amazing batting average (99.94 runs per innings) – he knew what bowlers were going to do before they'd even let go of the ball!

According to statistics, we'll have to wait another 6000 years for a cricketer to match Don Bradman's average.

SOME COMMON RULES OF BACKYARD CRICKET*

Any wicket. The batter can be run out at either end of the pitch. Useful when there is only one person batting.

Bat-for-ball. Whoever gets the batsman out takes the next turn at the crease. The drawback of this rule is that players who can't bowl or catch never get a chance to bat.

Can't go out first ball. A good rule for giving everyone a fair go, but it does mean that you can't bowl a hat-trick.

One hand, one bounce. If you catch the ball in one hand after it has bounced only once, the batsman is out. Very useful when there aren't enough fielders.

Six and out. If you hit the ball over the fence into the neighbour's backyard you score six runs but you're out. This rule helps avoid lost balls, and is particularly useful if your neighbour has a big scary dog.

Tippity-runs. You have to run whenever you hit the ball, no matter how far the ball goes. This one's good for making sure no one hogs the bat for too long.

*** WARNING!** These rules may cause arguments.

MASTERS OF DISGUISE

Of course, the best tennis servers and cricket bowlers are trying to stay one step ahead by disguising their body movements so that their opponents find it hard to predict where they will send the ball. They try to change the direction of the ball without changing the way they move their bodies. Next time you see Kim Cljsters or Glenn McGrath in action, check it out. Do their serving or bowling styles vary from one delivery to the next? We bet you can't spot it. The best players don't give much away.

GUESSING GOALIES

It's not just the little balls that fly too fast to keep an eye on. Professional soccer players can kick the ball up to 100 kilometres (62 miles) per hour. A penalty kick is taken only 11 metres (12 yards) away from the goalkeeper – that's only about 11 big steps. That means that the goal keeper has about .4 seconds to react after the ball has been kicked. The goal mouth must feel about as wide and hard to defend as the entrance to Luna Park.

In order to make a save, a goalkeeper needs to leap before the ball is kicked. Like tennis and cricket players, they look for clues that will reveal where the ball will fly. One trick is to sneak a peek at the opposing player's non-kicking foot. The kick usually goes in the direction that foot is pointing.

7

BEND IT LIKE BECKHAM

Soccer superstar David Beckham is famous for being able to curve the soccer ball around a wall of players, while still keeping it under the goal crossbar to beat the diving goalkeeper. Beckham would certainly get an 'A' for physics. When a soccer ball is kicked with spin, two forces give it flight. The *lift force* makes the ball curve. The *drag force* slows it down. How these two forces act together on the ball tell us where the ball will fly. When taking a 30-metre free kick, Beckham kicks the ball with great power. The ball begins spinning around and around like a top, then slows as it passes the opposition's defensive wall. If he kicks it just right, the ball starts to curl just as it passes the wall of players, making it very difficult for the goalkeeper to save.

TRAINING YOUR BRAIN

If you think that sounds way too complicated, try not thinking at all. Apparently, worrying too much about your technique actually makes things worse. Sports psychologists say that when you line up to kick a goal there are two different ways of thinking: one is called *internal focus*; the other, funnily enough, is called *external focus*.

Internal focus means you think about yourself and your own body movements. For instance, if you're playing Australian Rules football, your coach might tell you to 'watch the ball onto your boot'. If you do this, you'll be thinking about your technique; the way you move your arms and legs.

External focus is when you concentrate on what will happen after you've kicked the ball. For example, you might imagine how the ball will look flying through the air or through the goal posts.

BETTER OUT THAN IN!

It seems the ball is more likely to sail through for a goal if your thoughts have an external focus. This type of thinking works better partly because you don't confuse yourself

by trying to think about too many things at once.
Can you remember a time when
you missed a goal because
you couldn't stop
thinking about all the
tips the coach had
given you to improve
your technique?

Irish soccer star Robbie Keane had to
undergo surgery after injuring himself
while watching television. He damaged
cartilage in his knee while reaching to
pick up the remote control.

JONNY AND DORIS

Even English Rugby Union superstar Jonny Wilkinson once had problems with his kicking accuracy. So he decided to forget about technique and focus on 'Doris' instead. Now every time Jonny prepares to kick a goal, he 'externally focuses' on an imaginary woman called Doris sitting in the grandstand behind the goalposts. In the beginning, he visualised hitting her with the ball. As his kicking skills improved, he narrowed his target. First he pictured kicking a newspaper out of her hands, and now he's got it down to a soft-drink can.

2

IN THE SWIM

Australians love making a splash. We seem to be really good at anything that involves being in, on, or near the water. Australia won 16 gold medals at the Sydney Olympics in 2000 – five were for swimming, two were for sailing and one was for water polo. (Another was for beach volleyball, which almost counts!) Maybe it's not all that surprising; after all, we do live on an island.

STARRING AT STARTING

Surprisingly, what a swimmer does out of the water can make the difference between winning and losing. There are lots of different techniques for getting a flying start.

Libby Lenton is the Australian star of the short sprint events like the 50 metre freestyle. The whole race only takes about 25 seconds, so the way Libby explodes off the starting blocks is vital.

Believe it or not, back in the 1600s competition swimmers used to dive into the water bottom first!

Some swimmers like to hold the handles on the blocks, called a *grab start*. Others crouch down and look like they are about to start a running race rather than a swimming race. This is called a *track start*. Scientists have tried to work out which style is better. They haven't found a simple answer; both styles have their strengths and weaknesses.

The harder you push off the blocks, the further down the pool your dive you will take you. That seems like a good thing, right? But you actually have to spend longer on the blocks (we're talking tiny fractions of a second here) to generate the force needed to push you that bit further. So your opponent, who exploded off the block more quickly but with a little less force, might have got the jump on you. At this stage, scientists haven't been able to tell athletes which technique is better. It seems to depend on the height and size of the swimmer and the amount of time spent perfecting their diving technique. Just for the record, Libby Lenton uses a grab start, and she won bronze at the Athens Olympics.

IS SHAVING A SAVING?

Getting a good start is only one way for swimmers to reduce their times. You may have noticed that many swimmers, like Ian Thorpe, now wear black swimsuits that look as if they've been stolen from Batman's wardrobe. Scientists think that water slips more quickly past the suits than past human skin. This reduces *drag* and helps you to swim faster.

But not everyone likes to suit up. After all, it takes about 20 minutes to squeeze into a swimsuit like Thorpe's. Some swimmers shave all the hair off their bodies and heads instead. Australian sprint-swimmer Michael Klim is famous for his shaved head or 'chrome dome'. Removing all your body hair has the same effect as wearing a suit: water slips more easily past smooth hairless skin, which reduces your swim times.

Shaving is certainly a cheaper option. A full-length suit like the one Thorpie wears could set you back as much as $700! But unless you're very serious about your swimming, you probably don't need to bother with either. Shaving your body – or wearing the suit – only clips about three per cent off your time.

Snappy swimmers

A swimming coach in Darwin puts a two-metre crocodile in the pool while his young swimmers train. Forget shaving – can you imagine how fast you'd swim with a croc on your tail? (Luckily for the swimmers, the crocodile has its jaws taped together so it can't bite anyone.)

WATERLOGGED VAN WISSE

Have you ever felt exhausted after swimming one lap of an Olympic-size swimming pool? Well spare a thought for Australian swimmer Tammy van Wisse. In 2000–2001, Tammy swam the length of the Murray River. The Murray is 2438 kilometres (1515 miles) long, or the equivalent of 48 760 laps of an Olympic pool. Swimming each day and resting at night, Tammy finished her dip in 103 days and was estimated to have taken nearly two million armstrokes.

MONSTER MOTIVATION

Tammy specialises in 'ultra-distance' swimming. That means she's good at swimming really really REALLY long distances. She is the only person to have swum across Bass Strait. In 1999, Tammy swam the length of Scotland's famous Loch Ness – 38 kilometres – in the record time of just over nine hours. The average water temperature in the loch is near freezing, but even scarier for Tammy was the thought of the Loch Ness

Monster, which, according to legend, inhabits the deep black waters. No wonder she swam so fast!

So you want to be an ultra-distance swimmer?

ARE YOU PREPARED TO:

► Rub yourself all over with grease to keep out the cold?
► Risk hypothermia?
► Keep swimming even though you're throwing up from swallowing seawater?
► Swim in a cage to keep out the sharks?
► Lose 8–12 kilograms by the end of a race?

WINNING WOMEN

Did you know that women are better ultra-distance swimmers than men? Their secret weapon is a higher percentage of body fat, which comes in very handy for marathon swims. Here are some reasons why:

More in the tank. In the last stage of a long race our bodies break down fat and convert it to energy. More body fat means more energy to make it to the finish line.

A built-in wetsuit. A layer of fat acts as insulation against the cold – as blubber does in seals and whales.

Floatation aid. Fat helps you float, which means you can swim for longer without tiring.

Women are also said to be better at enduring pain than men, which is very helpful when you have to swim for days on end. Many athletic mothers have said that no amount of sporting agony can match the pain of giving birth. Just ask your mum.

Bodysurfing Barbie?

Scientists experimenting with the best way to bodysurf tried using Barbie dolls to test their theories. But Bodysurfing Barbie wasn't very useful; she just floats on the surface of the water.

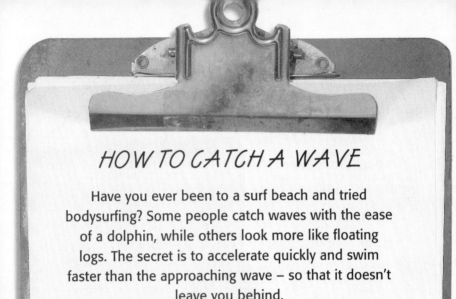

HOW TO CATCH A WAVE

Have you ever been to a surf beach and tried bodysurfing? Some people catch waves with the ease of a dolphin, while others look more like floating logs. The secret is to accelerate quickly and swim faster than the approaching wave – so that it doesn't leave you behind.

1 Begin in shallow water. It's much easier to get the necessary burst of energy by pushing off the bottom. You have to be a strong and fast swimmer to catch a wave in deep water.

2 Make like a dolphin. Take advantage of the wave's strength by diving through and out in front of it. It's called 'porpoising' because this is what

dolphins and porpoises do when they play in waves near the shore.

3 Choose 'arms back' or 'arms forward'. The 'arms back' style requires you to put your arms by your sides with your head up, popping out in front of the wave. If you want a longer ride it's better to choose the 'arms forward' style, pointing your arms out in front as if you were diving into a pool. But this means you have to put your face into the water and hold your breath!

4 Don't get dumped!

3

LIFE IN THE FAST LANE

The very first race of the very first modern Olympics, in 1896, was a heat of the 100 metres sprint. The race was won by Frank Lane of the USA in a time of 12.2 seconds. Today, competitors fly down the track even faster – men in just under, and women in just over, 10 seconds. The 100 metre sprint has become a favourite at the Olympics.

Asafa Powell of Jamaica and Justin Gatlin of the USA jointly hold the world record for the men's 100 metres sprint. They have both run the course in 9.77 seconds. Does this make them the fastest people on Earth?

Well, yes and no. It all depends on the wind factor.

Ever tried to run into a strong wind? It really slows you down, doesn't it? A wind blowing at your back does the opposite – it actually gives you a little push along. So if wind affects runners' times, how can we tell who really is the fastest runner on Earth? By using science and maths, of course!

Scientists have devised a maths equation that takes into account wind speed and direction so that we can compare results as if every race were run in the same conditions. If you take the wind factor into account, Maurice Green of the USA is actually the fastest human runner ever.

The equation looks like this:

$$T_0 = T_w \times [1.03 - 0.03 \times (1 - w \times T_w / 100)^2]$$

T_0 = corrected time, T_w = official time, w = wind assistance

A SMARTER STARTER

You've probably noticed that sprinters crouch down at the starting line to get a quicker start. It wasn't always like this. At the first modern Olympic Games in 1896, most sprinters started their races standing straight up, but the American team crouched down before the gun fired. This amazed and confused the crowds . . . and the other runners! Now sprinters don't just crouch down; they also put their feet against starting blocks.

This gives them something to push off from to get an even quicker start.

BOOTH'S BLOCKS

Do you know where starting blocks were invented? Australia! In the 1920s, an idea popped into the head of an Australian man called Charles Booth. He was a sprinter himself, but also an engineer. He and his running mates used to dig holes in the track (and in the lawn at home!) to push off from, but Charles thought there had to be a better way. He built the first starting blocks out of iron and used them at his local club. But officials thought it was cheating and banned him from running – for life!

By the 1930s, everybody was using starting blocks and Charles Booth's ban was lifted. He is still competing in sprint races at over 100 years of age.

At the World Masters Games in Melbourne in 2002, Charles Booth won the 100 metre sprint in a time of 28.57 seconds. He won the race comfortably because he was the only competitor in his age group.

A RUN TO THE DEATH

If you've got more staying power than speed, the 42-kilometre (26-mile) marathon might be for you. But why 42 kilometres? In 490 BCE, after a mighty battle at the town of Marathon, the Greeks overpowered an invading Persian army. The Greek commander wanted to send news of the victory to Athens as fast as possible. He wanted to know who could run the distance in the fastest time.

A Greek soldier called Pheidippides took up the

challenge . . . well, he was probably ordered to do it. Pheidippides ran like the wind to deliver the great news of the Battle of Marathon. When he finally reached Athens, he shouted, 'Rejoice, we conquer!' Then he dropped dead.

How far did he run? You guessed it – 42 kilometres. Even though things didn't turn out so well for the original runner, the modern day marathon celebrates this amazing feat.

Prod!
Prod!

Francisco Lazaro of Portugal collapsed from sunstroke and died of a heart attack during the marathon at the 1912 Olympics. He became the first athlete to die at the modern Olympic Games.

FIGHTING FIT

The marathon at the first modern Olympic Games in Athens was not a good one for Australia. Our only entrant was a man called Edwin Flack, who had already won two gold medals in shorter running races. With four kilometres to go, Edwin was winning the marathon, too. Then trouble struck. He was so exhausted that he began to zigzag across the road. A spectator ran over to catch him before he collapsed, but Edwin thought he was being attacked. So he punched the helper in the face!

Australia might not have done so well, but everyone was delighted when a Greek runner called Spiridon Louis won the first modern marathon in his home country. And unlike Pheidippides, Spiridon was around to celebrate afterwards.

A four-year-old Chinese girl called Gao Meng ran an entire marathon. It took her six hours, one minute and 10 seconds.

MARATHON MADNESS

The weirdest men's Olympic marathon took place in St. Louis, USA in 1904. During the race, a Cuban runner kept stopping to practise speaking English with people by the roadside. Another competitor was chased through a cornfield by two large dogs. The only place for the runners to get water was a well at the halfway mark; and the weather was so hot that more than half of the athletes collapsed! But the action wasn't over yet.

Fred Lorz of New York crossed the finish line first and was announced as the champion. But something fishy was going on. Officials soon discovered that Fred had hitch-hiked the last 20 kilometres! He had to give back his gold medal, which was then awarded to Thomas Hicks, also of the USA. Hicks had only survived the race by drinking whatever people gave him, including alcohol and raw eggs. He had to be helped across the finish line by officials. His winning time of three hours and 28 minutes is the longest in Olympic history.

DE CASTELLA GETS THE RUNS

In 1982, Robert de Castella of Australia won the marathon at the Commonwealth Games. During the race, spectators noticed him wiping the back of his legs with a wet sponge. Was he keeping his legs cool so that he could run faster? In fact, de Castella admitted

later that he'd
needed to go to
the toilet and had 'let go'
in the middle of the race.
He was using the sponge to
try to clean up the results.

FAINTING FEMALES

By now you might be wondering if the women's
Olympic marathon has as strange a history as the
men's. Well, until the 1984 Olympics in Los Angeles,
women weren't allowed to run the marathon at all.
Olympic officials thought the race was too tough for
the female body to handle.

At the 1928 Olympics in Amsterdam, a women's
800 metre race was held. That's two laps of the athletics
track. People were very excited because it was the
longest distance women had ever been permitted to
run at the Games. Some women ran so hard that they
collapsed after the finish line. When the officials saw
this, they insisted it proved that women weren't strong

enough to compete over any distance further than 200 metres. It didn't seem to matter to the officials that lots of men also collapsed after their races. So, for the next 32 years, the longest race for women at the Olympics was only half a lap of the running track.

Women were forbidden to take part in the ancient Greek Olympics altogether. In fact, married women weren't even allowed to enter the stadium to watch the events. If they were caught, the punishment was death.

Women were also banned from the first modern Olympics in 1894. Greek runner Stamata Revithi was furious that she was not allowed to compete in the marathon. She protested by running the marathon course the day after the men had run it. It took another

88 years before women were allowed to compete in the marathon at the Olympic Games.

In Paris in 1900, women competed in tennis and golf. Since then, the number of Olympic sports women take part in has been steadily growing. At the Olympics in Athens in 2004, 44 per cent of the athletes were female.

A BIG SECRET

At the 1936 Olympics, Stanislawa Walasiewicz of Poland came second in the women's 100-metres final. But Stanislawa wasn't happy with her silver medal – she thought she deserved the gold. She accused the winner, Helen Stephens of the USA, of being a man. Helen had to submit to a genital inspection that proved that she was a woman. But the story gets even stranger. Forty-four years later, Stanislawa was accidentally shot dead by a robber. When the doctors examined her body, they discovered that the silver medalist was actually a man!

4

THE WHEEL DEAL

If the bicycle had been invented in 490 BCE, things might have been very different for Pheidippides. If he could have jumped on a bike and pedalled to Athens he might have arrived in time to deliver the glorious news and then have morning tea.

Riding a bicycle is the most efficient way to travel. You can go five kilometres on a bike using the same amount of energy that it takes a car to move 85 metres.

The genius who invented the wheel probably lived around 6000 years ago. But, sadly for Pheidippides, it took another 5800 or so years before someone thought to put one wheel in front of another. The world's first bicycle was invented by a German called Karl von Drais in 1817.

Von Drais's bicycle was made entirely of wood (Yes, even the wheels!), and was called the Swiftwalker. Why not the Swiftpedaller? Because it had no pedals. To make it roll, you pushed the ground with your feet. To make it stop, you also used your feet – hard!

EVOLUTION OF THE BICYCLE

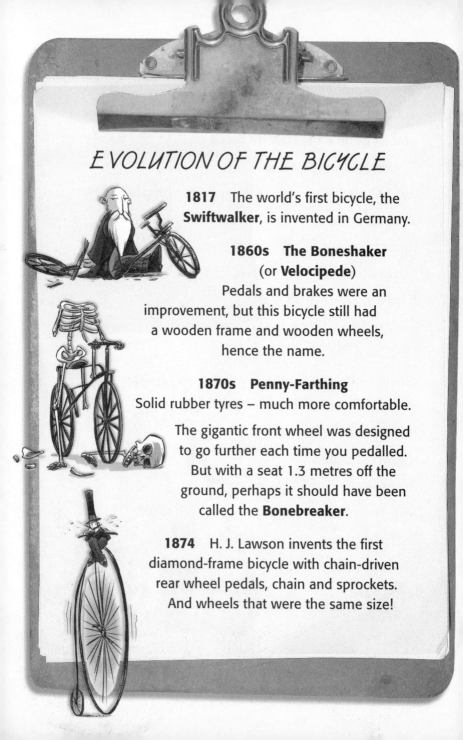

1817   The world's first bicycle, the **Swiftwalker**, is invented in Germany.

1860s   The Boneshaker (or **Velocipede**)
Pedals and brakes were an improvement, but this bicycle still had a wooden frame and wooden wheels, hence the name.

1870s   Penny-Farthing
Solid rubber tyres – much more comfortable.

The gigantic front wheel was designed to go further each time you pedalled. But with a seat 1.3 metres off the ground, perhaps it should have been called the **Bonebreaker**.

1874   H. J. Lawson invents the first diamond-frame bicycle with chain-driven rear wheel pedals, chain and sprockets. And wheels that were the same size!

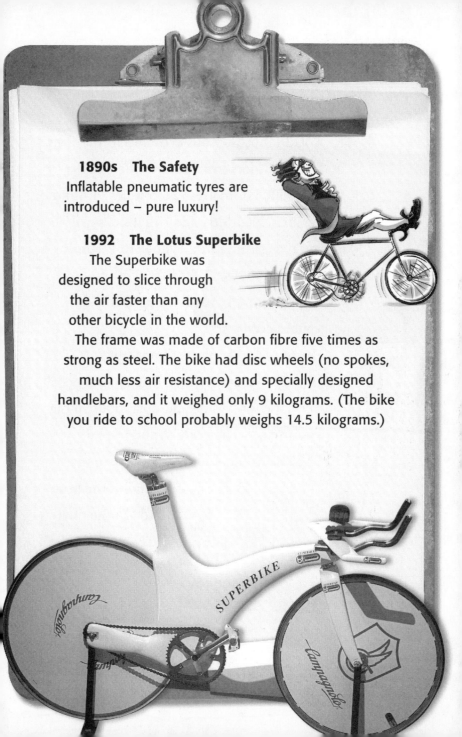

1890s   The Safety

Inflatable pneumatic tyres are introduced – pure luxury!

1992   The Lotus Superbike

The Superbike was designed to slice through the air faster than any other bicycle in the world.

The frame was made of carbon fibre five times as strong as steel. The bike had disc wheels (no spokes, much less air resistance) and specially designed handlebars, and it weighed only 9 kilograms. (The bike you ride to school probably weighs 14.5 kilograms.)

LE TOUR

The world's most famous cycle race is the Tour
de France. Riders from all over the world
travel 3500 kilometres (2175 miles) around
the French countryside – that's almost
as far as riding from Sydney to Perth.
The Tour began over 100 years ago, and in
the first race – on dirt roads – two-thirds of the
competitors didn't finish.

The modern race lasts three weeks,
with only two days of rest. The cyclists pedal
over flat countryside and up and down big
mountains. They ride through small
towns over cobblestone roads; in the
rain and in the heat;
and, on the final
day, through the
streets of Paris.

The cyclists ride up to 230 kilometres a day, and need lots of energy to keep going. They eat more than double the amount of food a normal person needs. The riders eat and drink about half of their day's rations without getting off their bikes.

8400 food bags and 42 000 water bottles are used by the cyclists during the Tour de France.

Four cyclists have won the race five times each. But the champion of champions is Lance Armstrong of the USA. He has won the race *seven* times in a row, from 1999 to 2005. What's even more incredible is that he did this after spending a long time in hospital being treated for life-threatening cancer.

Deep-sea cycling

An Italian mountain biker wearing a wetsuit and diving gear managed to pedal for 30 metres (33 yards) under the sea. His tyres were pumped up with water and his bike was weighed down with lead.

NATURE CALLS

If a rider has to go to the toilet during the race and doesn't have time to get off his bike he'll just pee out of the side of his cycling shorts while still pedalling! But if a leading cyclist needs to stop for a more serious toilet break, some of his team-mates will wait for him so that they can help him get back to the *peloton* (the main bunch of cyclists) as quickly as possible.

FORMULA FAST

If you think runners and cyclists are fast, wait until you hear what Michael Schumacher can do. He flies round the track at over 350 kilometres (217 miles) an hour. Of course, he does have some help, in the form of a Formula One racing car.

In the first official motor race, around 110 years ago, the winning car clocked up 16.4 kilometres (10.2 miles) an hour. Today, Formula One racing cars – the fastest cars in the racing world – reach speeds of nearly 370 kilometres (230 miles) per hour.

Formula One cars are an engineering miracle. They are made up of over 80 000 components. That means that if a car has been put together 99.9 per cent correctly, it would still start the race with

80 things wrong with it! Sensors inside the car monitor everything from tyre pressure to the temperature of the brakes, which can work in temperatures above 1000 degrees Celsius. Everything has to work like clockwork. And if it doesn't, it has to be able to be fixed in seconds by the pit crew during the race.

RACING CAR VS. FAMILY CAR

	Starting: Zero to 100 kph	Stopping: 200 kph to zero	How far on a tank of petrol?	How much?
Formula One car	3 seconds	55 metres	80 kilometres	Up to $500 million a year
Average family car	10 seconds	almost 300 metres	around 600 kilometres	Around $30 000 to buy

DRIVING YOU UP THE WALL

Formula One cars have almost as much in common
with planes as they do with the average family car
– they even have wings! Formula One wings work in
exactly the same way as plane wings, only in reverse.
They are specially designed to create 'down force'
instead of 'lift force'. This means that the pressure of
the air rushing past the car is pushing the car down
rather than lifting it up. The amount of down force
that the wings create when the car is driving really
fast is more than the car weighs. Scientists think it is
probably possible for Formula One cars to drive upside
down on the ceiling. No drivers have been too anxious
to try it, though!

'If everything seems under control, you're just not going fast enough.'
Racing car driver Mario Andretti

HOT UNDER THE COLLAR

If you think Formula One drivers have it easy, just sitting on their bums all day and being paid millions of dollars, you'd better think again. Driving a racing car is hard work. And it's dangerous. Since Grand Prix racing began in 1950, 75 drivers have died in races or at practice.

Racing around the track is also a pretty intense work-out. A normal resting heart rate is around 50–60 beats per minutes. Formula One drivers' hearts can pound at over 180 beats per minute for long periods. Their blood pressure also increases by as much as 50 per cent above resting levels.

Racing car drivers also become very hot and dehydrated during a race. The cockpit of their car can reach 50 degrees Celsius! The drivers have to wear a fireproof balaclava under their helmet, a long-sleeved fireproof vest under their overalls, and gloves. Drivers can lose as much as 5 litres of sweat during a race. Imagine what they must smell like at the end!

(It's true that they get paid millions of dollars, though.)

An earbashing

The noise in the driver's seat of a Formula One racing car can reach 125 decibels. That's as loud as a chainsaw, or like standing right in front of the speakers at a rock concert.

Scary stuff

If you're not afraid of high speeds, then the sport of skeleton might be for you. Skeleton competitors lie on their stomachs and ride a thin sled headfirst down a steep, 1200-metre-long track made of ice, reaching speeds of up to 130 kilometres per hour.

DOWNHILL DYNAMITE

Formula One drivers are pretty brave, zooming around the track at such terrifying speeds. But there's an Australian man who hurtles along almost as fast without wearing a seat belt. In fact, he doesn't even need an engine.

In April 2006, Michael Milton became the fastest ever Australian skier when he whooshed down a mountain at 213 kilometres (132 miles) per hour. Even more amazing is the fact that Michael only has one leg!

DON'T LOOK DOWN!

Speed skiing tracks are really steep. They have a gradient of 70 degrees. Standing at the top, is like looking over a two-kilometre-high cliff. Pretty scary! Michael accelerates at a rate similar to a Formula One car, going from zero to 100 kilometres (62 miles) per hour in about 3.2 seconds. He hits top speed about one kilometre down the mountain. Staying upright at that speed is like trying to stand still in a cyclone.

THE WILL TO WIN

Michael lost his leg to bone cancer when he was nine years old. The only question he asked the doctors when he heard the news was: 'Will I still be able to ski?' He competed in his first Paralympics when he was 14, won four gold medals at the 2002 Winter Paralympic Games, and in the same year was named the Sportsperson of the Year with a Disability. Michael recently retired from ski racing with a whopping 23 Paralympic and World Championship medals under his belt.

Extreme shopping

An elderly man drove an electric shopping cart for ten kilometres along one of Britain's busiest highways. His speed was clocked at 8 kilometres per hour.

IS IT A BIRD? IS IT A PLANE? NO, IT'S DONALD CAMPBELL

Donald Campbell lived life in the fast lane. In 1964 he set a land speed world record in his super-car, which was called *Bluebird*. Guess how fast he was going?

648 kilometres (403 miles) per hour! At that speed, he could have driven from Melbourne to Perth in just over five hours – that's only an hour more than it takes to fly! Three years later, Donald swapped his super-car for a super-boat and tried for the water speed record. He got his boat up to 480 kilometres (298 miles) per hour, then . . . tragedy. His boat somersaulted from the water and smashed into thousands of pieces. His body was never found.

ALL ABOUT THE OLYMPICS

The Ancient Games

The Olympic Games began in Ancient Greece around 770 BCE. Only young men who spoke Greek were allowed to compete.

Events included wrestling, boxing, running, discus, javelin and chariot racing.

Athletes usually competed naked – partly because the weather was so hot and partly to celebrate the human body.

The winners didn't receive medals but were crowned with a wreath of olive leaves.

The Olympic Games were outlawed in Greece in 393 CE by Theodosius I, Emperor of Rome.

The Games were named after Mount Olympus, the mountain where the Greek gods where said to live.

The Modern Games

The Olympics have taken place every four years since 1896, except for 1916, 1940, and 1944 when competition was suspended because of war.

In 1924, the Winter Olympics was held for the first time. The Olympic Games now includes the Winter and Summer Games.

The period of four years between each Games is known as an 'Olympiad'. Each Summer Olympics is referred to by the number of Olympiads since the first Modern Games.

250 athletes competed at the first modern Olympic Games. Around 11 100 competitors from 202 countries competed in the 2004 Olympic Games in Athens.

The first Paralympics (Olympic Games for athletes with a disability) was held in Rome in 1960. The name comes from the Greek word *para* meaning 'alongside'. The Paralympics are held 'alongside' the Olympics every four years.

5

CHEATERS VS. WORLD BEATERS

Athletes are always trying to run faster, jump higher, lift bigger weights and break world records. If they can't do it naturally, some of them resort to taking drugs or using other methods to improve their performance.

before   after!

This is illegal and is called *doping*. The term comes from an alcoholic drink called *dop* that Zulu warriors would gulp down to make themselves fight bravely in battle.

Are athletes dopes for taking drugs to make them perform better? We reckon they are, because sporting drugs can be very bad for you – and getting caught using them can get you banned from competition for life!

Old-fashioned cheating

Almost 3000 years ago, athletes at the Ancient Olympic Games would eat and drink 'special' foods to help them win. The foods included extracts of mushrooms and plant seeds. At the Olympics in 776 BCE, some athletes ate sheep testicles as a source of extra testosterone – the first anabolic steroid!

BUT THAT'S NOT ...COOKED!

DO YOU WANT TO WIN OR NOT?!

TAXI!

Have your muscles ever ached or felt like they were burning from too much exercise? Well, imagine how sore the muscles of marathon runners or triathletes must get after competing nonstop for hours and hours. Even when their muscles are screaming for rest, they must struggle on to the finish line.

In order to keep working, muscles need plenty of oxygen. But how do we get oxygen from the air in our lungs to our muscles? We have blood vessels! Blood vessels are the roads and highways of our body. They are full of red blood cells that are like taxis for oxygen. Red blood cells pick up oxygen at our lungs and zip it off to exercising muscles.

The more oxygen there is in our muscles, the more energy we have to exercise. Lots and lots of training makes our bodies more efficient at delivering oxygen to our muscles. But some athletes use illegal methods to boost the amount of oxygen reaching their muscles. This is called *blood doping.*

BLOODY CHEATS!

If you have more blood in your body, you also have more red blood cells swimming around. Some long-distance athletes actually add 'extra' blood to their own bodies. This is called *blood boosting.*

57

But where does this extra blood come from? Often, it is donated by someone else. This can be very risky because an athlete might catch an infection from the other person's blood. At the Olympic Games in 1984, seven American cyclists jammed extra blood into their bodies to help boost their performance. They won nine gold medals between them, but several cyclists also got sick. Since then, blood boosting has been banned at most competitions and is considered cheating.

E-REE-THROW-POY-EE-TIN

That's how you pronounce *erythropoietin*, or EPO for short. What is EPO? It's a hormone that our kidneys produce that tells our body to make more red blood cells.

Scientists can now make synthetic EPO in their laboratories. This artificial EPO was invented to help doctors fight diseases. Unfortunately, some devious athletes have put this synthetic EPO into their own bodies to boost their red blood cell count. And, as you know by now, more red blood cells means that more oxygen can be carried to an athlete's pumping muscles.

MEGA MUSCLES

Powerful muscles are very important in sports like sprinting, jumping, gymnastics and weightlifting. If you train a lot, or lift weights, you'll notice your muscles getting bigger and stronger. Our bodies help by producing a hormone called *testosterone*. Testosterone stimulates our muscles to make new proteins so that they grow bigger. The more testosterone we produce, the bigger our muscles grow. Men have more testosterone than women, which is part of the reason why they have naturally bigger muscles.

Elite athletes train incredibly hard, often every day. But, for some of them, that's not enough. Scientists have discovered how to create artificial molecules that act like testosterone. These molecules are called *anabolic steroids* and some athletes take them to speed up the growth of their muscles.

The side effects of anabolic steroids can include acne, stunted growth and depression. They can make men bald, and women grow beards. Steroids can even affect your personality, making you angry, aggressive and violent. Worst of all, many athletes who take steroids will end up with heart and liver disease from using them. These diseases can sometimes be fatal.

At the Sydney Olympics, 24 athletes were kicked out for using steroids.

I'M TRYING!

An Australian Rugby League player came off the ground after a game in 30-degree-Celcius heat. He was asked to pee in a bottle to see if he was taking any sporting drugs. But he was so dehydrated that no pee would come. He drank many litres of juice, but still no pee! So the Drug Control Official had to go home with the player and wait until he gave a pee sample. Finally, five hours after the game had finished, at 1.30 in the morning, the player could go to the toilet. He had not been doping, by the way!

SPECIMEN
Clean!

WELL, IT WAS A LONG FIVE HOURS - BUT WE GOT IT!!

61

HOW TO CATCH A CHEAT

1 An athlete is asked to provide a urine sample in front of a tester who is of the same gender. The tester witnesss the urine sample going from the athlete's body into a container.

2 The athlete also has a blood sample taken in the presence of a Drug Control Official.

3 The athlete is responsible for their urine and blood samples until they are sealed in a sample collection kit.

4 The athlete pours a measured amount of their urine sample into two containers – one labelled 'A' and the other labelled 'B'.

5 A drug-testing laboratory analyses part 'A' of an athlete's urine and/or blood sample for the presence of any prohibited substances or doping methods.

6 If container 'A' returns a *positive* test result (indicating that cheating may have occurred), the athlete has the right to have container 'B' analysed to double-check the positive result.

TOP FIVE EXCUSES
FOR FAILING A DOPE TEST

1 Swedish athlete Ludmila Engquist claimed her husband had put anabolic steroids in her food because he was angry with her.

2 German runner Dieter Bauman insisted that someone had put steroids in his toothpaste.

3 After being caught for steroid doping, British bobsledder Lenny Paul claimed: 'I have eaten spaghetti Bolognese; there must have been hormones in the meat.'

4 American Cyclist Tyler Hamilton was caught for injecting extra blood into his body, but his wife explained that his dog had died from a blood transfusion and therefore Tyler would never do such a thing.

5 When Australian cricketer Shane Warne was caught using a banned sporting drug he blamed his own mother!

THE WHIZZINATOR

The World Anti-Doping Agency has reported that some athletes have used a fake penis in an attempt to fool drug testers. The gadget, called *The Whizzinator*, releases a 'clean' urine sample at the press of a button.

A clean result

In 1994, shot-putter Paul Edwards drank a whole bottle of shampoo before a drug test in an attempt to cover up the positive results.

6

DYING TO WIN

If you think that playing sport is all fun and games, think again. Have you ever twisted your ankle playing netball? Have you ever been kicked in the shins at soccer? How about getting cuts and bruises from footy or hockey? We bet you can answer 'yes' to at least one of these injuries. It's true – sport can be bad for your health . . . even *deadly*!

SPEED KILLS

75 Formula One drivers have died in crashes since 1950, but car racing can also be dangerous for the spectators. During the famous *Le Mans* race in France in 1955, Pierre Levegh was hurtling along at 240 kilometres (149 miles) per hour when he clipped the car next to him. His car spun out of control and flew into a grandstand packed with people. The car exploded into a ball of flames, killing Pierre and more than 80 spectators.

Sideline shenanigans #1

One soccer fan got so angry during a game that he threw his mobile phone at a referee – it broke the poor guy's nose.

SORRY? WHAT?!!

LE TOUR EST DANGEREUX

Three cyclists have died while riding the Tour de France and a fourth drowned during a rest day. But the riders are tough – they know the dangers and they still love the race. Sometimes they just don't know when to stop . . .

On 13 July 1967, the sun was shining down on the Tour. In fact, the temperature was more than 40 degrees Celsius (104 degrees Fahrenheit)! But the poor cyclists had to keep riding. And to make matters worse, they had to pedal to the top of the steep Mont Ventoux.

About three kilometres (1.9 miles) from the top of the mountain, a British rider called Tommy Simpson toppled from his bicycle. Spectators sprinted to his aid. Exhausted, Simpson muttered, 'Put me back on my bike.' So the spectators helped him back onto his seat. Simpson pedalled away but began swerving all over the road. About 200 metres (219 yards) further on, he collapsed again. This time he did not get up. He died on the way to hospital.

GET READY TO WINCE!

It's not always the extreme sports that turn out to be deadly. Vladimir Smirnov won an Olympic gold medal for fencing in 1980. But two years later, he had a horrible accident. During a bout at the World Championships, his opponent's sword snapped. Part of the sword stabbed through Smirnov's face-mask, pierced his eyeball and entered his brain.

NO, REALLY! I'M OK!!!

He died nine days later, just as the championship was drawing to a close.

DOWN IN A BLAZER OF GLORY

In 1999, Owen Hart, a pro wrestler known as The Blue Blazer, was making a grand entrance before one of his wrestling matches when everything went wrong. As he was being lowered into the ring from high up in the roof, his harness malfunctioned and he fell 24 metres (26 yards) into the ring. The Blue Blazer was dead minutes after he hit the ground, but the crowd thought it was all part of the act and cheered as he was carried out by paramedics.

Sideline shenanigans #2

In the 1983 U.S. Tennis Open, a linesman was smacked between the legs by a tennis ball served at great speed. The linesman grabbed his groin and toppled backwards off his chair. In the fall, he smashed his head against the ground and broke his skull.

A REAL HEART-STOPPER

It's not just athletes and spectators who take a risk – being a coach isn't all fun and games either. Take Jock Stein for example. Jock was the manager of the Scottish soccer team. In 1986, his team was playing Wales, trying to qualify for the World Cup. Scotland only needed one goal to make it, but they just couldn't score. Then, in the final minutes of the match – GOAL!

They did it! All of Scotland rejoiced. But the stress was too much for poor old Jock – he had a heart attack and died on the field.

A Brazilian cyclist was run over by a plane as he tried to cross an airport runway.

MASCOT MAYHEM

Have you ever dreamed of dressing up in a big padded suit and parading up and down in front of thousands of people? Maybe you want to be the big cat at the footy, or the big phoenix at the netball. Be warned – it's not as easy as it looks to be a mascot.

The suits are very hot and heavy and the person inside often gets dehydrated, and sometimes ends up in hospital. Mascots fall over a lot; they twist their ankles and hurt their knees. Some mascots have fallen down stairs. Herky the Hawk – the mascot of the University of Iowa, in the USA – even had two bones in his back broken when a fan hit him with a giant, blow-up banana.

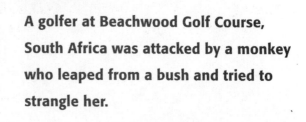

A golfer at Beachwood Golf Course, South Africa was attacked by a monkey who leaped from a bush and tried to strangle her.

TUG OF WARRRRGGGGHHHH!!

Two men had their arms ripped off in a tug-of-war contest. Both men wrapped the rope around their left arm to get a better grip. But the rope snapped and so did their limbs. Doctors operated for seven hours to re-attach their arms.

Sideline shenanigans #3

A man in England was so distraught when his favourite soccer team lost a big game that he couldn't go to work. His doctor wrote him a sick note that said he was suffering from 'football trauma'.

7

HAVE YOU GOT WHAT IT TAKES?

Do you dream of growing up to be a sports star? If reading the last chapter didn't put you off, then you've probably got two of the most important qualities a sportsperson can have – guts and determination. Maybe you want to captain the Australian netball team, like Liz Ellis. Or win Olympic gold medals, like Ian Thorpe and Cathy Freeman. Or maybe even play for the Socceroos in the World Cup, like Harry Kewell. Whatever sport you play, here

are a few tips to help you on your way to becoming
a superstar.

BE A KEEN COUCH POTATO

Next time your parents tell you to turn the TV off and
go out and play, tell them you're too busy training.
It's true! Watching expert athletes play your favourite
sport actually can help you improve your own skills.
This is called 'modelling' or 'observational learning'.
Just by observing closely you can pick up tips on your
technique. Listening to the expert commentators can
also help direct you towards what to watch out for.

Television gives you replays and freeze frames that highlight the important aspects of a skill. Watching the cricket is a good example of this, because there are lots of close-ups and replays of Shane Warne bowling his leg spinners or Ricky Ponting hitting a cover drive.

Hot and steamy

To get ready for the hot weather predicted for the Rome Olympics in 1960, Englishman Don Walker exercised in his bathroom with the heaters turned on and kettles boiling. He won the 50 kilometre race walk.

PRACTICE, PRACTICE, PRACTICE

Unfortunately, sitting on the couch is not going to get all the work done. You have to get out there and play as much as possible. Our bodies learn to do things by repetition, so you can improve your skills and reflexes by practising, practising, practising.

GOT A SPARE TEN YEARS?

Interviews with elite athletes from around the world, and in a wide range of sports, have shown that most of them took at least ten years of training in their sport to make it to the top. In Australia, players in the Australian netball, basketball and hockey teams spend an average of 12 years and approximately 4000 hours practising their sport before they make it to the national team.

MIX IT UP

Most Australian sports stars played a variety of sports when they were at school. For example, Llyeton Hewitt played Australian Rules football almost as well as he played tennis.

Playing a number of sports improves your overall coordination and fitness, and gives you a much better chance of finding the sport you love.

USE YOUR HEAD

A player's success isn't always measured by the number of goals they score. In team sports, it also matters how good you are at reading the game. That is, knowing where the ball and the players are all the time, and being able to predict the play.

For many players, reading the game is as difficult as reading a book in a foreign language. But if you're good at it, like netballer Sharelle McMahon or footballer James Hird, it can make all the difference. It's not enough to work on your body; you have to train your mind, too.

Three-year-old Peruvian girl Sofia Figueroa swam 1000 metres in 48 minutes without stopping. The only instruction her coach gave her was to lift her head up to one side to breathe.

GO FOR YOUR LIFE

According to Australian government recommendations, you should do at least 60 minutes of vigorous activity every day. It helps you grow strong bones and muscles, increases your flexibility and even helps your posture. Being active can also boost your confidence, reduce stress and help you relax. Even if you don't have the makings of an elite athlete, you can still have fun and keep fit by playing sport. You can play at school, in local clubs, in the backyard or in the park with your mates. You might not make it to the middle of the MCG, but you could end up doing something really cool – like becoming a sport scientist!

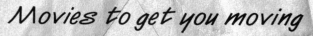

Movies to get you moving

Cool Runnings (bobsled)
The Mighty Ducks (ice hockey)
Field of Dreams (baseball)
Bend It Like Beckham (soccer)
Rocky (boxing)
Chariots of Fire (running)
Like Mike (basketball)
A League of Their Own (baseball)
When We Were Kings (boxing)
Hoosiers (basketball)
The Karate Kid
Shaolin Soccer

IT'S TRUE! SPORT STINKS

You have between two and four million sweat glands spread over the surface of your body. When you get hot, your sweat glands exude a liquid that's mostly made up of water, salt and fatty compounds. When the sweat evaporates it cools you down.

If a marathon runner didn't sweat during a race, their body temperature would rise approximately one degree Celsius every three minutes. By the time they reached the finish line, the runner's body temperature would have hit about 80 degrees Celsius! (Although they probably wouldn't have made it to the finish line because nobody can survive for very long with a body temperature over 45 degrees Celsius.)

If you're exercising heavily on a hot day, you might lose around two or three litres of sweat every hour. Pretty stinky, right? Well, sweat itself doesn't have an odour at all. The smell actually comes from the bacteria that live on our skin and feed on our sweat.

QUIZ YOUR MATES

How many dimples are there on a golf ball?
Usually 336.
But there can be anywhere from 300 to 500.
Scientists fiddle with the number, trying to make the
ball fly further. The dimples are not always round either.
Some scientists think that hexagonal dimples make a
golf ball fly further.

How big was Phar Lap's heart?
6.25 kilograms.
The average weight of a horse's heart is 4.2 kilograms.
An champion American horse called Secretariat had a
BIG heart – nearly 10 kilograms!

How many stitches are there on a baseball?
108 double stitches.

**How many golf clubs are professional players
allowed to carry in their golf bag?**
14 clubs.

What is the longest kick in AFL history?
105.5 metres.
Fred Fanning of Melbourne booted this massive
drop-kick in 1939.

What was Sir Don Bradman's batting average?
99.94 runs.
Graeme Pollock of South Africa is second, with an
average of 60.97 runs.

How short was the shortest Major League baseballer?
109 centimetres.
In 1951, Eddie Gaedel batted for the St. Louis Browns.
He batted only once and received a walk. It was too
hard for the pitcher to throw a strike because Eddie was
so small. He even wore a uniform with the number
$1/8$ on the back!

How old was the youngest ever Olympic athlete?
10 years old.
Dimitrios Loundras from Greece competed in the
gymnastics in the 1896 Athens Olympics.

How old was the oldest ever Olympic athlete?
72 years and 280 days old.
Oscar Swahn of Sweden competed in shooting
and won a silver medal.

**In badminton at the Olympics, how many feathers
must the shuttlecock have?**

14 feathers.

JUSTIN KEMP and DAMIAN FARROW
teamed up at university when they were studying
to become sports scientists. They talked about
sport better than they played it, so they began
a radio show called 'Run Like You Stole Something'.

Damian now works for the Australian Institute
of Sport where he teaches coaches and athletes
how to train and play better. (If your favourite
netball or football team loses, it might be his fault!)

Justin is puny, so he wanted to learn more
about how muscles work during exercise.
He studies them in his science laboratory and
he still works on the radio where people can't see
his own scrawny muscles.

HEATH McKENZIE has illustrated more books
and magazines than he can count on two hands
and feet. He has also enjoyed an illustrious sporting
career – the greatest highlight being the time he
needed a full knee reconstruction after his first
and only game of mixed netball. Suffice to
say, he prefers to watch rather than play and
suspects he'll just stick to drawing!

THANKS

Thanks to the Australian Catholic University, Paul Rovere, 3RRR FM, the Australian Institute of Sport, Andrea Farrow and Jack Kelaher.

Justin Kemp and Damian Farrow

The publishers would like to thank istockphoto.com and the photographers named for images appearing on the following pages: Stefan Klein (clipboard and torn notepaper used throughout text); pages i & 65 Jaimie D. Travis (girl caught in skipping rope); page 2 Nathan Watkins (tennis ball); page 4 Tom Brown (cricket ball); pages 8 and 11 angelhell (soccer ball); page 21 Nicholas Belton (headless doll); page 29 Kenneth C. Zirkel (stopwatch); page 41 Michael Gatewood (bike helmet); pages 44 and 46 Alexander Mikula (speedometer); page 49 Adam Waliczek (ski boot); page 52 blackred (laurel); page 59 Mark Thompson (measuring muscle); page 61 Renaud Gombert (pills); page 71 Diane Diederich (flattened by a football) and Stefan Klein (photo frame); pages 71 and 72 Michael McCloskey (bandaids); page 79 Jonas Staub (trophy); page 80 Doug Miller (popcorn), Brian Powell (tickets) and Monika Wisniewska (boy with soccer ball). Thanks also to Paul Rovere for the photograph of the Lotus Superbike on page 39.

THE MODERN SUMMER OLYMPIC GAMES

Year	Host city	Country
1896	Athens	Greece
1900	Paris	France
1904	St. Louis	United States
1906	Athens	Greece
1908	London	United Kingdom
1912	Stockholm	Sweden
1920	Antwerp	Belgium
1924	Paris	France
1928	Amsterdam	Netherlands
1932	Los Angeles	United States
1936	Berlin	Germany
1948	London	United Kingdom
1952	Helsinki	Finland
1956	Melbourne	Australia
1960	Rome	Italy
1964	Tokyo	Japan
1968	Mexico City	Mexico
1972	Munich	West Germany
1976	Montreal	Canada
1980	Moscow	Soviet Union
1984	Los Angeles	United States
1988	Seoul	South Korea
1992	Barcelona	Spain
1996	Atlanta	United States
2000	Sydney	Australia
2004	Athens	Greece
2008	Beijing	China
2012	London	United Kingdom

WHERE TO FIND OUT MORE

Books

Brasch, R., *How did sports begin?*, Angus & Robertson, Sydney, 1995

Farrow, D., & Kemp, J., *Run Like You Stole Something*, Crows Nest NSW, Allen & Unwin, 2003

Farrow, D., & Kemp, J., *Why Dick Fosbury Flopped*, Crows Nest NSW, Allen & Unwin, 2006

Postman, A. & Stone, L., *The Ultimate Book of Sports Lists*, New York, Bantam Books, 1990

Wallechinsky, D., *The Complete Book of the Olympics (2004 Edition)*, London, Aurum Press, 2004

Websites

• www.exploratorium.edu/sports
Sports science activities, exhibitions, news and links

• www.ais.org.au
The Australian Institute of Sport

• faculty.washington.edu/chudler/experi.html
Neuroscience for kids, lots of different experiments and activities that test your brain and body

• en.beijing2008.com
The Bejing Olympic Games, 2008

• www.athletics.org.au/education/
Athletics Australia's website for kids

• www.formula1.com/insight/
Formula One, includes technical and scientific information

• www.letour.fr
The Tour de France

• www.netball.asn.au
Netball Australia, includes links to your favourite clubs

• www.footballaustralia.com.au
The Football Federation of Australia, includes all the latest news about the Socceroos and the Matildas

• www.afl.org
The Australian Football League, includes links to your favourite clubs

• www.nrl.org
The National Rugby League, includes links to your favourite clubs

• www.rugby.com.au
Ruby Union, includes all the latest news about the Wallabies

• www.cricket.com.au
Cricket Australia

INDEX

Australian Rules
football 10, 77, 82
Armstrong, Lance 41

Beckham, David 8–9
bicycle, evolution of
37, 38–9
blood boosting 57–8
blood doping 56–7
body surfing 22–3
Booth, Charles 27–8
Bradman, Don 4, 83

Cambell, Donald
50–1
cheating 27, 31,
54–64
cricket 4, 5, 6, 7, 63,
76

De Castella, Robert
32–3

erythropoietin 58

fencing 68
Formula One
1, 43–7, 49, 66

golf 35, 72, 82

Hewitt, Lleyton 77
Klim, Michael 16
Lee, Brett 4
Lenton, Libby 14, 15

marathon 13, 28–33,
35, 56, 81
mascots 71–2
Milton, Michael
48–50

netball 65, 71, 74,
77, 78

Olympic Games 13,
15, 24, 26, 29, 30,
31–2, 33–5, 52–3,
55, 58, 61, 68, 74,
76, 83, 86

Paralympics 49, 53
Pheidippides 28–9,
30, 36, 37

Roddick, Andy 1–2

shaving 16–17
skeleton 48
soccer 6–9, 11, 65,
67, 70, 73, 74

starting blocks 26–8
steroids 60, 61, 63
swimming (pool)
13–17
swimming
(ultra-distance)
18–21

tennis 1–3, 4, 6, 7,
35, 70, 77
testosterone 55,
59–60
Thorpe, Ian 16, 74
Tour de France 40–1,
67–8
training 7, 9–11, 17,
57, 59, 60, 75–8
tug of war 73

Walasiewicz,
Stanislava 35
Warne, Shane 63, 76
Wilkinson, Jonny 12
wind resistance 24–6
women at the
Olympics 33–5
world record 24,
48–9, 54